"I read it from start to finish in one sitting ch story resonating with the joy of life, unique celebration of the in These send-offs will make you I want to go out in style?"

~ Patti Wade, contributing author,
Chicken Soup for the Soul

"Celebrating the life of loved ones after they have passed does not have to be a serious and somber affair, as attested by the delightful stories Susan Opalka shares in **Going Out in Style**. Her book offers creative and meaningful alternatives inspiring healing and joy to the individuals who want to prepare their own final affairs as well as the loved ones who will honor and fulfill them."

~Holley Kelley, M.S., C.P.G., F.T., Gerontologist,
Author of *Sunrises and Sunsets: Final Affairs Forged with Flair, Finesse, and FUNctionaltiy*

"The way we honor and celebrate the life of someone who has died is taking on new and very individual forms. Boomers are not content with the rote services of our parents and are looking to participate in how our loved ones send us off. **Going Out in Style** is a joy-filled expression of how some of us have custom-built highly personal tributes. It is a wonderful read and a trove of inspiration for those of us who are getting closer to the finish line."

~ Marian Lindholtz, M.I.M. Professional Writer

"As an Art Therapist, Grief and Bereavement Counselor and Counselor Trainer, I continually witnessed the ways in which the utilization of ritual can be key to helping people honor the lives of those whom they had loved and lost. This book explores the need to give voice to personal loss, and it is filled with moving portraits of individuals striving to celebrate the essences of those whom they still continue to miss after death. Through these heartfelt examinations, the book also highlights the creative and expressive ways in which each person has chosen to share his or her own story. These personal accounts embrace the intricacies of life, love, loss, and remembrance and provide an initial glimpse into the subsequent journey to healing. This must-read is a celebratory gift; it is caring and respectful and is filled with a sense of joyous inspiration.

~ Gail F. Jarson, M.A., Visual Artist, Retired from
Art Therapy and Counseling

Going Out in Style

A Collection of Personal Celebration-of-Life Stories

Susan Opalka

Robert D. Reed Publishers

Bandon, Oregon

Robert D. Reed Publishers
P.O. Box 1992
Bandon, OR 97411
Phone: 541-347-9882; Fax: -9883
E-mail: 4bobreed@msn.com
Website: www.rdrpublishers.com

Cover Designer: Cleone Reed
Book Designer: Susan Leonard

Softcover ISBN 13: 978-1-944297-20-6
eBook ISBN: 978-1-944297-21-3

Library of Congress Control Number: 2017937963

Designed and Formatted in the United States of America

Table of Contents

The Home Front **75**

Part Two: The Guide - How to Create a Personal Celebration of Life

How to "Go Out in Style" **91**

Appendix:
Example of a Personal Celebration-of-Life Plan.... **105**

About the Author **117**

Introduction

When I was young, funerals were a somber event. I was raised Catholic Italian in the Midwest where funerals were a three-day affair. The deceased was on display in a large room at the local funeral home, and the family was "on call" to receive guests from 10:00 a.m. to 8:00 p.m. The room was typically lined with chairs and flower arrangements. (People and families who knew the departed were expected to send a floral arrangement based on how close they were to them. Neighbors, business associates, and not-so-close family sent small bouquets, while those friends and family members closer to the person sent large flower arrangements from huge baskets to free-standing flower structures. This could get very competitive, and the relatives would all go around reading the cards on the flowers to see who spent the most money.) And the sickening sweet smell of flowers stayed in your nostrils and brain for several days after.

Everyone was to wear black clothes— suits, dresses (no slacks or pant suits allowed for females!), and most of the older women usually had some type of lace veil on their heads. There was a lot of sobbing and wringing of handker-chiefs. Laughing was absolutely not acceptable; even smiling was frowned upon. At 7:00 p.m. a prayer or rosary was said and everyone was expected to participate. This all took place for two days with the church mass followed by a cemetery burial on the third day. After the cemetery trip, everyone went back to the family home, and people brought enough food to feed a small town. The crying, sobbing, weeping, and handkerchief-wringing went on for all three days, including the last gathering at the house to share food.

My parents have both passed on and my brothers and sister and I gave them the funerals they expected – serious, solemn and respectful – which they clearly deserved and would have appreciated. I, on the other hand, do not want any part of that! I want my "going out" to be joyous and even fun. I sincerely believe that many Baby Boomers and younger generations *do not* want the send-off that we gave our parents or grandparents. We want to go out in style – our own personal style.

This book is a collection of non-traditional, personal celebration-of-life stories which I hope will inspire you to do something truly meaningful for yourself or for someone you love. It is also a guide to help with this celebration including all the information you need to create your plan.

Part One: The Stories

Outside Venues

The Bonfire Beach Party

Kenny was a wild party guy. Everyone loved Kenny and he made friends everywhere he went. When he walked into a room, a bar, or a restaurant, people knew he was there—always laughing and telling jokes. When Kenny was around, the atmosphere always turned into a party. Even in the coldest days during Wisconsin winters, Kenny would come in with his Hawaiian shirt bringing cheer and beer.

Every 4th of July, Kenny and his wife Cheryl, high school sweethearts and married 38 years, would hold their Annual Bonfire Beach Party on the beach of Lake Michigan. It started out small with a few friends and family, and over the years it blossomed into a "regular" crowd of 60 to 65 people of all ages. On the day of the party, they'd begin the bonfire at 3 p.m. while bringing in BBQ grills, tables, kegs, and enough food and drinks to feed an army. Four tables were needed just to hold the desserts! They'd play horseshoes, volleyball, swim, dance, play cards, and party until dark. When it was dark enough, they would break out the S'mores and end the evening by shooting off the fireworks. Everyone looked forward to this party all year long.

One night in May when Kenny was coming home from the drugstore, he was hit head-on by a truck trying to pass a car. He was taken to the local hospital where he died shortly after. Cheryl was completely distraught, yet she felt the best way to honor Kenny was to hold their Annual Bonfire

Beach Party for his memorial service, so she re-created the July beach party – playing and singing all of Kenny's favorite songs. When it got dark, his ashes were mixed in the fireworks display. Everyone cheered, drank, and saluted him. He would have loved his send-off party! Cheryl said they are going to continue to hold the Beach party each year as his legacy.

Sailboats at Sunset

It took Melissa and Jeremy almost twenty years to finally save up enough money to buy their sailboat. It wasn't very big, a 17-foot WindRider Trimaran sailboat, but it was all theirs! Since they both worked, they had limited time when they could sneak away and go sailing. Their favorite times were at sunset where they could just relax and enjoy the water, the scenery, and each other's company. They solved all of their problems and also the rest of the world's problems on those sails! Their last sail together was on their anniversary when they brought a picnic basket with champagne, their favorite Mediterranean beef & veggie wraps, and red velvet cupcakes for dessert.

When Jeremy was killed in a bizarre accident on the construction site he was supervising, his body was cremated. Melissa kept his ashes in a container on the living room mantle. She knew what she wanted to do with his ashes but couldn't find what she was looking for. It took her four months and hundreds of garage, estate, and close-out sales; but she finally found five pharmaceutical/medicine bottles with corks. She invited her mom, his mom, his dad, and his sister to join her on the small sailboat. They each wrote a message to Jeremy, telling him how much they loved him. Each message, along with some of his ashes, was placed in a separate bottle. They launched the boat almost at sunset and sailed out to their favorite area. When the sunset was just right, they all kissed their bottles and put them into the water. The five bottles stayed together for a long, long time.

It was hard to leave, but they all felt good about what they had done.

The Porsche 911 Carrera S Cabriolet

Heather was absolutely crazy about her 911 Carrera S Cabriolet Porsche! It was her pride and joy – a midnight blue metallic convertible with 6 speeds. This all started in high school when she saw her first Porsche 911 and fell in love with it. All through college she continually talked about graduating, finding a great job, and buying her Porsche. This was her major goal, and she never lost focus or changed her mind.

And her dream actually came true! She graduated with a degree in Accounting and found a really good job with a local mortgage company. For three years, she scrimped and saved and finally, close to her 25th birthday, she bought her Porsche 911 Carrera S Cabriolet dream car. She would put the top down and cruise around town waving to all her friends. Everyone recognized her and her car and knew where she was by where her car was parked.

When Heather drowned in a boating accident, her parents knew she wanted to be cremated and sought the help of her three lifelong friends, Jenna, Megan, and Chloe in spreading some of her ashes. Following the Memorial Service, Heather's friends placed the open container of ashes in the front seat of her Porsche; and they drove all around town, driving by all her old "stomping grounds": her favorite pizza place, restaurants, bars, hair and nail salon, Washington Middle School, and the ballpark where she played softball in high school. They had a running dialog with "her" in the car, telling her which places they were visiting. By the time that they got back to her home, her ashes were all gone.

Heather and her dream car Porsche had their final ride together.

The Last Trail Ride

Travis's Grandpop was a trail blazer who lived all his life out west on a ranch with acres and acres of riding trails. His main ranch house, barns, and stalls were all built in the 1920's. When Travis was younger, he and his eight cousins would spend their entire summer vacations with Grandpop and Grammy. They would ride horses and spend hundreds of hours with him creating and maintaining horse trails during the day. At night, they would settle down in sleeping bags under the stars at one of the several campsites. During their trail rides, they would usually end up at one of the campsites where Grammy would be waiting with a camp-fired dinner followed by a marshmallow roast. Those trail rides and campsite events are still considered to be the best times of Travis's life.

Grandpop wasn't a big guy. He was small, wiry, and strong as an ox, actively involved with the ranch and working the horses. Perhaps that's why no one ever really thought of him as being old. When he passed away, Grammy wanted his burial and memorial to be out on the ranch land. The whole family gathered and decided to give him his Last Trail Ride. His casket was put on a horse-drawn cart, and everyone rode horses in a procession out to a special trail that led to a gravesite newly created for him. After they buried him, each of the family members found a rock from the area and, with colored markers and paints, they painted and wrote out their special thoughts and words to him. The little kids painted, drew pictures, and added glitter and stickers to their rocks. The rocks were then sealed with polyurethane to protect them from the weather. They surrounded his grave with all the decorated rocks. The trail is called the "Grandpop Memorial Trail".

Whenever Travis comes to visit Grammy, he rides out to see and talk to Grandpop in his special place.

The Dog Park

Doug and Ginny adored their two bull dogs, Bubba and Bruno. They'd pamper them with special treats and take them to the dog park twice a week during the weekdays, and at least once on the weekends. About a year ago, the neighborhood was blessed when the city decided to refurbish the old elementary school property a couple blocks away. It's now an administration building for the school system, and the run-down playground was turned into a wonderful neighborhood dog park. It's fenced in, has some great trees, benches, and a giant grassy area for the dogs to run and play.

This dog park is one of the most popular places in the neighborhood. Neighbors leave messages and share information, i.e., new restaurant openings, local coffee-bar coupons, car-pool opportunities, homes for sale and rent, garage sale flyers, dog and babysitters wanted, etc. at the park's posting station. Those who go to the dog park regularly have become close friends with one another.

Since Doug and Ginny take Bubba and Bruno to the dog park every Tuesday, Thursday, and Saturday, they became friends with others who go those same days. They'd all talk about their dogs, their kids and grandkids, jobs, and life in general. Many of the "Saturday People" meet for coffee or drinks after their walks and a few of the "Friday People" meet for beers at the tavern down the street.

When Doug passed away in June, Ginny posted an invitation to all the dog park neighbors to attend a short memorial service at the park on the Saturday following his passing. Twenty chairs were set up under the big tree and everyone gathered around. Ginny passed out a flyer which had Doug's photo on it and a poem he had written about their bull dogs. There were about 30 people who came. Those who knew Doug well talked about their experiences with him and the dogs. The gathering lasted about 45 minutes, and at the end, Ginny handed out little bags of dog treats to all the attending dogs. She also sprinkled a few of Doug's ashes throughout the dog park, since that was where he would want to be.

The Fisherman

Marie's husband Carl was a quiet, shy man. He didn't speak much and never wanted the spotlight or to be the focus of the conversation. He was always willing to give others the attention and was happy to be the supportive audience. He would sit back, listen, and smile. Some people say Carl was a "kindred spirit" because, while he didn't speak up, he was always there to help everyone; and one time gave someone the shirt off his back! They live in a very small town near a lake in Ohio where everyone knows everyone. Many families have lived in and around this town for generations.

When Carl died, Marie wanted to do something that was very personal, but low-key for Carl. He would not have wanted a big public service or ceremony with a lot of hoopla. Carl really loved fishing. He learned to fish from his father and grandfather and was "hooked" from the time he was five years old. All his life, his happiest times were when he was fishing, either alone or with his fishing pals. They would fish after work, on weekends, and even on holidays if they could get away with it. So Marie felt it seemed only fitting that his memorial and final resting place would be in or near the lake.

Marie's children were on board with her lake idea and helped her plan to make his memorial a reality. After a short church service with only family attending, his close fishing friends and families were invited to his memorial celebration which was held on the dock at the lake. They all reminisced about Carl's life and his pals told some stories Marie had never heard before. She heard tales of the times they all ditched high school and went fishing, the time they had a hole in the boat and almost drowned, etc. They shared good laughs before scattering Carl's ashes into the lake. After that, they went to the Bait House, which was a small place with fishing gear and supplies on one side, and a small café on the other side. Everyone was served the Daily Special (the Bait House dedicated the meal to Carl and named it "Carl's Special").

Marie's daughter, who is very artsy crafty, took several of Carl's fishing lures and added beads and a ribbon to each and created Christmas ornaments and earrings out of them. Each of Carl's friends were given one to take home and hang up or wear.

Marie felt that Carl was smiling down during his quiet, but personal celebration.

Amazing Desert Sculptures

Celia's parents, Eileen and Gino, moved their family to the Sonoran Desert in the 1950's. At that time, almost all of Phoenix, Arizona was a desert! She and her brother Enzo grew up on a Wild West ranch, and their childhood friends included all the ranch animals and horses, along with the desert creatures such as lizards, scorpions, horned toads, roadrunners and snakes. They loved this desert, Wild West

environment and it clearly influenced their lives and careers. Celia's passion and career is painting desert land-scapes which she displays and sells in a small, local gallery; and Enzo, after traveling the world in his 20's, settled back in Arizona. For the past several years he has been a successful ceramic artist who specializes in Western sculptures.

Their parents died a couple of years ago; and Enzo and Celia kept their ashes in a nice urn but didn't really know what to do with them. They had been discussing this issue for a while and finally found the solution. They both knew they wanted to honor their parent's love of the desert, and they also wanted something physical which would be a last-ing remembrance. So Enzo designed an amazing sculpture in the shape of a giant horned toad! He mixed their parent's ashes into the clay and glazes, creating a bright, festive, colorful sculpture which sits as the focal point of their desert garden. This way, their mom and dad can always be in their beloved desert, and their presence will live on for many years to come.

Motorcycle Club

Even though Billy was in his 60's, he still thought of himself as a teenager. He bought an old Harley motorcycle when he was about 17 and spent most of his life in and around the motorcycle culture. For the past twenty-five years, he belonged to a family-friendly motorcycle club. There were about 40 club members from all walks of life: doctors, teachers, bar owners, accountants, mechanics, etc. The president of the club was a licensed plumber. They all had a love of bikes and family. The wives would organize parties, picnics and potlucks each month, while the kids would run around and play together. Many of the motorcycle club's rides and events were sponsoring local community charity organizations. When the club members went on their motorcycle rides, they all wore their red and black t-shirts. It was quite a sight to see them all rumbling down the roads!

One day Billy was riding home on his bike and was struck by a van making a left turn. Billy died instantly in the street. The whole club closed ranks around Billy's family and gave them the financial and emotional support they needed. The wives sewed special patches on their club t-shirts in remembrance of Billy. At his outdoor memorial, all the club members wore their special red and black t-shirts and released hundreds of red and black balloons in memory of Billy. It was a spectacular sight! It was captured by everyone's camera phone and sent viral within seconds. They all have copies of that moment in their phones, in their vision, and in their hearts.

Billy will truly be missed.

Birthday Trail

Dana's sister Lindsay was an outdoorsy gal. She loved anything and everything as long as it was outside. She walked, hiked, ran, jogged, climbed, and camped every chance she got. Lindsay felt that nature was the perfect environment and spent as much of her time in the woods and mountains as she could. She held a trail hike each year on her birthday, and Dana, along with several of Lindsay's friends would spend the day with her hiking along the river. Their trail ended at the adjacent park where her mom and two aunts would be waiting with all the picnic food and supplies. They would eat, have birthday cake, and then make plans to do it again next year. Even after Lindsay was diagnosed with lymphoma, in between her treatments when she had

stretches of being fairly healthy, she and Dana would walk the river trail whenever they could.

After Lindsay died, Dana, her mom and Lindsay's friends, took her ashes and spread them along her "birthday trail". Dana also worked with the County Parks Department and made arrangements to have a park bench dedicated to Lindsay. She purchased a plaque with Lindsay's name on it, which was attached to a bench located at the end of the trail. Dana still walks the trail along the river each year on Lindsay's birthday, and when it's ended, she sits on "Lindsay's Bench" and talks to her. Dana believes Lindsay knows she's there.

The Dachshund Lover

Phil and Julie and been lovers and breeders of Dachshund dogs forever. They raised their kids and dogs together, and when the kids left home, the dogs got their total attention. Their house was full of everything with Dachshunds on it – pictures, small figurines, large statues, blankets, coffee mugs, towels, and even an entire set of glasses with matching bowls. Their whole lives revolved around their dogs. Between breeding, grooming, dog shows, and the Annual Weiner Race, they had no other free time. If you wanted to visit Phil and Julie, it would depend on the dogs' schedule! All their friends learned to head out to the local dog shows if they wanted to spend any time with either of them.

Even when Julie became ill, they still focused their lives on the dogs. Julie wouldn't have it any other way. She slowed down a bit and handed over the breeding, grooming, and dog shows to Phil and their son Phil Junior; but she would not give up the Annual Weiner Dog Race. The last time Julie attended the race, she was in a wheel chair with an oxygen tank attached. Still, she cheered her "babies" on and enjoyed every minute of the race.

After Julie died, Phil had some of her ashes put into tiny containers and attached them to the collars of her Dachshunds. Now, she is always close to her "babies" and she continues to cheer them on during the races and be a part of it.

Occupational Options

The High School Drama Teacher

In a small town in the Northeast, the local high school drama teacher passed away. She had just recently retired; and her family wanted to honor her life and her commitment to both the high school's drama program, and also to her many years of participation in the local Community Theater productions.

After much thought about where to have her memorial service, the family decided to rent out the old "Uptown Theater" which had been quite the movie house in its day. They rolled out the red carpet and invited everyone who was touched by her. This would include all her high school students from the past thirty-two years, and all her Community Theater actors and stage crews.

When the attendees (audience) arrived, they were given a "playbill" which featured her photo and a short biography. There were large bouquets of flowers placed on the stage, along with a podium and two large, poster-sized photos of her sitting on tripods. After her grandson, as the family spokesperson, welcomed the audience, several of her past students came to the podium and told their stories of how she had inspired or helped them. Many of her friends, family members and community folks came up on stage and told of the wonderful and humorous experiences they had with her over the years.

Finally, after all the speeches were over, the lights were dimmed, and the large movie screen came down. At this time, the audience watched a 10–12 minute "newsreel" of her life and all the plays she directed. The last frame was a picture of her smiling face. And when the lights came up, everyone gave her a standing ovation and applauded!

It was a wonderful and positive tribute to her.

World Traveler

Stephanie and Kelly had been airline attendants for almost fifteen years. They met when they started their training for the same airlines. After a couple of years, they each went their different ways, and then ironically, they ended up back together several years later, along with two other gals who trained with them – all working for the same international airlines. They had the best time travelling to foreign places together. Needless to say, they had seen much of the world. They used to say how lucky they were to have experienced the world's countries and cultures. Every international trip brought a new excitement, even if they'd been there before. Outside of work, the four of them would meet for dinner and drinks whenever they were all in the same city.

Unfortunately, Stephanie died last year after complications from a bout with pneumonia. Her only living relative was her grandmother, so there was a small service at her grandmother's church. Stephanie's written wishes were to be cremated, so Kelly asked her grandmother if she would share some of Steph's ashes with her and her friends. They told her grandmother about their plan – that each of them would take some of Stephanie's ashes with them on their international trips and scatter them in all the places and cities that she loved. Stephanie's grandmother thought it was a great plan.

As of today, Stephanie "resides" in several parks, gardens, fountains, bridges, and castles all over the world.

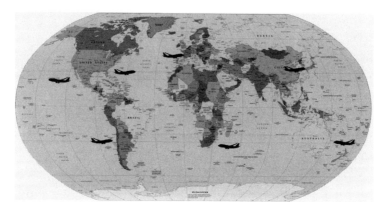

Famous Vince

The local pastry chef, Vince, was famous. Well, famous in Joe and Kathy's "Little Italy" neighborhood. Vince grew up in the neighborhood and never left. His family ran the Italian restaurant off Barton Street, and Vince created all the desserts. Ever since he was young, he always wanted to be a pastry chef, and his parents were very patient and encouraging during his early years of experimenting. Over time,

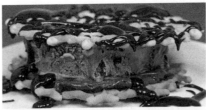

he developed into a well-known, reputable, and much-sought-after pastry chef (he really *was* famous).

Joe and Kathy had been going to Vince's family restaurant for about eight years and always thought it was their own special secret. Apparently, many others thought the same thing! People would drive all across the city to have some of Vince's desserts. After eating a wonderful Italian meal, most customers would order two desserts — one to eat there, and one to take home. He was famous for his double chocolate biscotti and his ricotta pie; however, Kathy's favorite was his anisette cookies.

The news of Vince's sudden death shook the entire restaurant community, especially the pastry, bakery, and dessert people, who are a pretty close-knit group in their city. They know and respect each other's talents despite being competitors. Outpourings of grief and support came from all over. Everyone wanted to honor Vince in some way. Vince's

parents finally decided to have a personal family-only church mass and private funeral, but also a public reception.

The reception was a two-day affair that was held at the family restaurant. All of Vince's desserts were presented in a huge buffet that included homemade gelatos of all flavors, breads, tiramisu, cream layer cakes, pizzellas, cannolis, ricotta pies, biscotti, and a vast assortment of his special-recipe cookies. There must have been several hundred people who tasted and toasted for two days.

The family is now working on a memorial cookbook with all of Vince's dessert recipes; and once it is completed, the proceeds will all be given to Vince's favorite neighborhood Boy's and Girl's Club.

The Coach

Louie was the baseball coach at the local community college for over 30 years. Coach Louie was the mainstay and the backbone of the sports program, and was also a major part of the institution. All the students, whether they were part of the athletic program, a sports team or not, knew and loved Coach Louie. Coach Louie never had a bad word to say about anybody. He loved his job and he loved his students and team players. The college had tried for years to promote Louie to the Athletic Director position, but he always refused the job. He said it would put too much distance between "his kids" and him. The baseball team never won any major championships, no state titles or conferences, but everyone in town wanted to play for Coach Louie.

When Coach Louie passed away, his family gave him the traditional funeral, but they also held a special memorial service for him on the college's baseball field. On a non-game Saturday, the family invited his current and past students, athletes, and assistant coaches. The word spread, and over 500 people showed up on the field and in the bleachers! Families whose kids he coached years ago came, along with half of the faculty and student population. There was a microphone set up at the pitcher's mound, and many of his current and past students gave tributes to him. They told how he motivated them to be the best they could be, not only in sports, but also in life. It was heartwarming to hear all the stories. The family ordered a six-foot baseball-themed cake from the local bakery which was placed on tables at home plate to share with the crowd. They also served the classic baseball game drinks – water, lemonade, and Gatorade.

The best part was at the end of the service when Louie's grandkids ran around the bases spreading some of his ashes. Afterward, they brought out several large baskets full of baseballs with "Coach Louie" stamped on them and passed them around. When you walked away with one of Coach Louie's baseballs, you definitely considered yourself a winner!

Renaissance Ryan

As a child, Ryan's favorite books were all about knights and castles. He made swords and shields out of any material he could find and begged his parents to drive for hours to the closest Renaissance Festival every summer. His best friend, Ben, got roped into all his sword fighting and jousting contests; and when they were about 12, they created their own "coat of arms." When they were in high school, Ryan talked Ben into joining the Society for Creative Anachronism with him. This is an international organization that re-enacts the dress, arts, skills, and heraldry of pre-17th century Europe. Because of Ryan's passion for this, he eventually influenced several other friends into being members of SCA's Middle Kingdom. While the Society offers equestrian weapon combat, rapier (fencing), martial arts, and other activities, Ryan and his friends focused mostly on archery and started the first Archery Club at their high school. Every summer during their high school years, the boys wore medieval clothing and participated in annual SCA royal courts, celebrations, contests, feasts, and tournaments.

After graduation, Ryan joined the Army and was determined to continue his "combat and chivalry quest" to protect his country. He was in Afghanistan for 18 months when he was killed by an IED. After his church service and traditional military funeral, his local SCA group decided to hold their own medieval banquet in his honor. During high school, the basement in Ben's house had been the official meeting place for the group members, using an old picnic table as their meeting and "banquet" table. In Ryan's honor, they arranged an archery tournament, ordered a take-out dinner which was their "feast", and dressed in their medieval clothing. They kept the "Throne Chair" at the end of the table empty for him in his honor, and toasted him throughout the feast.

Although the guys have now scattered and are no longer active members of the Society, they added Ryan's initials to their shields as a remembrance.

Favorite Things

Dixieland Style

Nadine's Grandma Jane (known to family members as G.J.) was born in New Orleans; and even though she had not lived there for over forty-five years, Louisiana was still a big part of her life and personality. Throughout Nadine's growing-up years, her grandma told her stories about the culture, the food, and the music of New Orleans. G.J. played the piano on an old Steinway upright at all of their family parties and holidays. Most of the songs she played were jazz or Dixieland; she especially liked the Dixieland ones. G.J. also liked Cajun food of all kinds, and made sure her shrimp creole dish was served at every family gathering, even Thanksgiving!

When G.J. passed away last year, the family wanted her memorial service to be "New Orleans Dixieland Style." One Friday night the family rented out the small side of the  local VFW hall and hired a Dixieland band. The musicians wore the traditional white pants, striped coats, and those straw hats you see in old photos. While they played Dixieland jazz songs, such as "When the Saints Go Marching In," "Basin Street Blues," "Down by the River," and many others, the family served a buffet of all the Louisiana Cajun foods G.J. talked about and loved all her life. There was crawfish, pork boudin, shrimp creole, gumbo, jambalaya, and of course, rice and beans. Nadine and her cousins wore strands of purple, green, and gold beads, and danced to the jazz music in honor of G.J.

Classic Car Club

Dick and Linda have been members of the local Ford Car Club for as long as Bob and Kris can remember, and they have been members for over 30 years. The Club is now down to about 25–30 members, as some members moved away over the years. The Car Club consists mostly of husbands and wives who have owned or still own Fords.

The Club meets once a month on a Saturday night in the sales room at the local Ford Dealership. Some of the members have old classic Fords, some have new ones; one couple has an old Edsel. At the meetings, they talk about each other's restoration projects, trips they're taking with their cars, local car shows they can attend (to show off their cars, of course), and mostly they decide where they're going to eat after the meeting! They publish a monthly newsletter which documents all their travels and restoration projects.

Besides their meetings, they have potlucks, picnics, and make the rounds of local diners. Sometimes they all drive their cars in a procession to car shows in towns two to three hours away. They all enjoy meeting new people who have interests similar to theirs. They recognize birthdays once a month with cakes and cards, and try to help each other when there is a need. If someone needs help on a big repair or restoration, several members will jump in.

When Dick became ill, Bob and the Club made sure his project stayed on track; and when he passed away a few months ago, Kris and the other wives were right by Linda's side. When Linda asked the members to be a part of his memorial service, they all readily agreed. After the church service, twenty Fords drove in a procession out to the cemetery. Bob and Kris searched online and found an old restored Ford hearse to carry Dick's casket. It was so unusual that the local paper published a photo of the procession! Certainly, it was on the front page of the Club's newsletter, and they all know that's just how Bob would have liked it.

It was such a great memorial that all the Ford Car Club members decided they wanted the same thing done for them when their time comes.

The Ballerina

Marcella was an average fourteen-year-old girl. She was attached to her new cell phone, and she enjoyed going to the mall with her girlfriends. They never spent much money; they just liked to wander in and out of the stores to see the latest fashions and designs. And, oh yes, meet with the boys from her school at the food court.

Many of her girlfriends were on soccer teams, but Marcella was totally passionate about ballet. On most week days after school, her friends would practice soccer and she would practice ballet. On Saturday mornings, her friends would head to the soccer field while she went to the ballet studio. They would all meet up later on at the mall. It was a pretty good plan and worked well most weeks.

Because the soccer games, her ballet recitals, and all the practices seemed to be at the same time, they never really got a chance to cheer each other on. After a few years, Marcella had adjusted to having two sets of friends: her school soccer friends and her ballet studio friends. She was really close to her ballet friends too, but since they all lived in different parts of the city, the only additional time they spent together was to celebrate their birthdays which were held at the studio.

Marcella was an intermediate/advanced dancer and had just finished a Master Ballet Intensive when she died of a brain injury she incurred in an automobile accident. Both her soccer and ballet friends came to her church service; in fact, it seemed like most of her junior high were there. Her parents were grateful for their attendance and the huge number of cards, flowers, and stuffed animals given by all the young people. For some reason, however, they felt like they still needed to do more for Marcella.

So, a couple months later, when it would have been her fifteenth birthday, they brought a cake decorated with a ballerina to the ballet studio for a party to celebrate her life. At the party, her parents gave away all her leotards, ballet shoes, hair ribbons and tiaras, along with dozens of costumes and sequin tutu's she had worn at competitions. They also set up a ballet scholarship in Marcella's name. Once that was done, they finally felt they had fulfilled their tribute to her.

Purple

Jeannie was Monica's best friend. They'd been best friends for the past twelve years. Both of them have children who live in other states; and since they didn't see them often, Jeannie and Monica became each other's "family". They celebrated birthdays and most holidays together, along with their book club gals. The Sisters' Book Club gals did something together every week: either a lunch out or at someone's house, going to a movie, scouring the library or estate sales for good books, or field trips to the symphony, museums, or the mall. After so many years together, they all knew each other really well.

After a doctor's appointment, Jeannie was diagnosed with stage-three cancer. She kept up the weekly activities with her friends for as long as she could, but eventually the cancer got the best of her. When Jeannie died, her daughter Lucy and her husband Rob came to make the final arrangements. They gave Jeannie a very respectful and dignified service at a local funeral home. While the service was very nice, it seemed pretty generic to Monica and the Sisters' Book Club gals, because Lucy really hadn't been around her mom very much in the past several years, and really didn't know her favorite things as well as they did.

That's why the Sisters' Book Club decided to give their own "Jeannie Memorial." The remaining seven book club gals went to Jeannie's favorite restaurant. They all wore something purple, which was Jeannie's favorite color; they all ate carrot cake which was her favorite dessert, and they all told their favorite Jeannie stories. They had her favorite purple flowers (violets) as the centerpiece on their table – actually it was seven small violet plants -- and then at the end of their celebration, each one took home a plant to keep in memory of Jeannie.

Whiskey and Sweet Potato Curly Fries

Craig was an attorney in a downtown law office in a large southwest city. While he was pretty well-known in the legal community for his litigation skills, he was more well-known at Donnelly's Sports Bar just a few blocks away from his office. In fact, he was what they called "a regular", since he spent most evenings there either cheering on one of his favorite sports teams, or just spending time with his friends. He had his own table and was teased about "holding court" most nights. If his friends needed him and couldn't reach him on his cell phone, they knew to call Kevin Donnelly at the bar.

Unbeknownst to all of his friends, Craig had stage-four testicular cancer. Some of his friends had noticed that he looked thinner and was less energetic, but they never suspected he was dying. When Craig didn't show up for a week at Donnelly's, Kevin called Craig's law firm looking for him. Kevin was told that Craig had died of cancer five days earlier and that his funeral service and burial would be in Southern California where his family lived. Because Craig was a single guy, his friends didn't have contact with his family; therefore, none of his local friends were invited to his services.

It seemed really dark and dreary at Donnelly's for about a week until someone suggested that the bar should have their own memorial for Craig. Maybe that would cheer everyone up! The word was spread and all the "bar regulars" were invited, including Craig's friends from his law office. They had a "Craig Happy Hour" on Friday and served Donnelly's Special Sub Sandwiches, Craig's favorite sweet potato curly fries, his special draft beer, and shots of his favorite Jameson's Irish Whiskey. They danced, drank, and told Craig stories. After several hours of drunken toasts, laughing, crying, story-telling, and a whole lot of curly fries, they felt they had given Craig a great party to celebrate their friendship with him.

They knew he would have had a great time at his party.

The Amber Box

Nothing could be more tragic than when a seemingly healthy infant dies for no apparent reason. Todd and Jenny were looking forward to spending a lazy Saturday at home with their ten-week-old daughter, Amber, and her two-year old brother, Griffin. But they were not prepared for what was to come. When they checked on Amber that morning, they came to the horrific realization that she was not breathing. At that moment, their lives were changed forever. Their hopes and dreams for Amber were gone.

For months, they tried to make some sense of it all, but were given no clear answers to this tragic event. While Jenny and Todd felt they were not novice parents, they made themselves almost physically ill trying to think of what they did wrong. Words like "Sudden Infant Death," "unpredictable," and "unexplained" were all used. They were grief-stricken, riddled with guilt, and just could not move forward.

Their friends, filled with sincere concern and sadness, tried to find something to do that was meaningful, and a way to help Todd and Jenny get through this heartbreak. They gathered up some of Amber's baby items – Baby Book journal notes, photos, a necklace, booties, a pink and white knitted cap, and her Minnie Mouse binky.

They arranged and secured all of the items on pink velvet and placed them into a newly made shadow box with a glass top. When the "Amber Box" was completed, they presented it to Todd and Jenny. While they felt they had done something important for them, they were also afraid it might backfire and cause more grief.

Todd and Jenny were amazed at how wonderful this gift was. It contained all the little things that represented Amber in one place. They were truly thankful to their friends for their love and caring. This was just what they needed.

Griffin asked that the shadow box be hung in his room so he could talk to Amber at night. Now, when Todd or Jenny reads Griffin his nighttime story, Amber hears it too.

Scrapbook Addicts

Scrapbooking can be a fun activity, or it can be an intense addiction. In one case, it was clearly an addiction. There were four friends who had been scrapbook addicts for the past several years. Individually, they had always been somewhat crafty all their lives. Even before they knew one another, each had been actively involved with some type of craft: macramé, origami, stamping, beading and jewelry making, mosaics, home-made greeting cards, Christmas decorations – whatever it was, one of them had tried it and had hundreds of examples to prove it! When scrapbooking became the next "Big Thing," they all ended up meeting in a class to learn this new craft/hobby. They immediately became the Scrapbook Addicts.

That was about six years ago. They enjoyed being together and met regularly to learn about new tools, techniques, and materials, and to share ideas. Once, they drove four hours to a Scrapbooking Convention to see what everyone else was doing. They created scrapbooks for their children, grandchildren, and friends with elaborate embellishments to record the special events in their lives.

When Maggie died suddenly after a routine knee surgery, the other Scrapbook Addicts realized they had created scrapbooks for everyone in their families and most of their friends, but none of them had a scrapbook for themselves! The three of them went to work and, with the help of Maggie's family, created a Maggie Book that documented her life. This included her childhood, wedding, and family life; but it also contained a huge number of physical examples and photos of many of the crafting projects she created throughout the years. They gave the book to her family who absolutely loved it. In fact, her grandchildren made a video of it and put it on Facebook so they could share it with everyone who knew Maggie.

It was truly emotional for the Scrapbook Addicts, as the video was titled "Cherished Moments of Maggie through the Eyes of Her Scrapbooking Friends."

Texas Line Dancers

Texas has long been known for its love of country western music and dancing. There are hundreds of dance groups all over the state; even Lea's small town has at least a half dozen groups. Lea's local line-dance group has been together for more than 22 years. They've weathered each other's divorces, marriages, good and bad children and grandchildren, and celebrated most special occasions together.

When Lea's good friend Dee passed away, her children arranged a very serious and formal service at her Bible church, followed by a reception in the church basement. It was the typical powdered-lemonade drink and ginger-cookie fare that they'd served for the last hundred years in that basement. While Lea felt the service was sweet and honored Dee, she thought the reception was rather boring and really did not represent the Dee she knew.

Lea's line dance group was very polite and told Dee's children they appreciated all that was done for their mother, but would they object if Lea's dance group held their own memorial. With the children's permission, they created their own celebration for Dee.

The dance group held the memorial during one of their weekly dance get-togethers and played all Dee's favorite country songs, and danced all the line dances she liked best (actually, Dee had taught the group most of them).

They set up tables with red and white checkered table-cloths, and put a pair of her polished cowboy boots on each table with a handful of red and white roses in them as decorations. They served BBQ chicken and pulled-pork sandwiches, cowboy beans, and Dee's favorite dessert of strawberry shortcake.

It was loud. And fun. And full of music, dancing, and laughter. It was just what Dee would have wanted.

A Tree for Manny

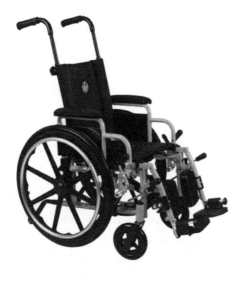

He started Kindergarten in a wheel chair, but other than that, Manny was a typical kid. He loved to take photos and create videos on his smart phone, play internet games, and build cities on Mindcraft. No one, including Manny, seemed to mind or think anything of his wheel chair. For the next six years, he was just like any other student. He did homework, wrote book reports, participated in spelling bees, and worked on class projects. When it came to the outdoors, however, he was limited, as he was born with a genetic lung disease and often had difficulty breathing. He sat outside in his wheel chair during recess, and his friends sometimes included him in minor ball throwing and catching games.

While he was in the seventh grade, his chronic infections increased and his lungs deteriorated. He passed away shortly after winning first prize at the seventh-grade science fair where he displayed an interactive computer-oriented photosynthesis plant life-cycle.

At Manny's middle school, there were four seventh-grade classes and they all wanted to do something to honor and remember Manny. The teachers asked for ideas and ended up with several options. The students voted and chose to plant a tree at the school in his memory. But it didn't stop there. As all seventh graders were required to take an art class during the year, they decided that each student would make a 4" x 4" ceramic tile with his/her own colors, designs, decorations, and signatures for Manny. Throughout the year, all the finished tiles were created and "fired" with a long-lasting glaze. At the end of the year, the one-hundred-plus tiles were adhered onto a concrete base and Manny's parents donated a flowering tree which was planted into the base.

They had a "Manny Tree-Planting and Dedication Ceremony" in the courtyard on the last day of school. The tree and the colorful, creative planter is a lasting memory of a colorful, creative young man—Manny.

The Golf Course

Ronnie was 62 years old when he died of a heart attack on the golf course. Ronnie loved to play golf. It was his passion. It was his obsession. Therefore, it was very appropriate that his Celebration of Life was held at the Country Club's golf course.

A few years ago, Ronnie and Barb bought a patio home on the second tee of the Club's grounds. Ronnie would go over on the weekends and have breakfast at the club, then hang around looking for someone to play golf with. He would play whenever he could. With his friends, by himself, or with strangers. He was always available when someone needed a partner or they needed a fourth member for a team. During the weekdays, Ronnie was a successful financial analyst, but when he got home, he made time to play a few holes, hit at the driving range, or just practice his putting.

One Saturday morning, Ronnie left to play golf and never came home. Barb got a call that he had been taken by ambulance to the local hospital. He didn't survive the night. Barb was dumbstruck because he was so young, but she was happy that he died doing what he loved.

It just seemed right to have his celebration at the Country Club, and the people there were very cooperative and supportive. They all loved Ronnie too. They held a special breakfast reception for Ronnie, and all his golf buddies and club members came. They arranged a long table with photos of Ronnie playing golf, a large flowering centerpiece containing miniature golf clubs, and had several glass bowls of black golf balls with Ronnie's name printed in gold so that each friend and member could take one home. Barb also passed out packages of black golf tees with Ronnie's name printed in gold on the package. Every person said it was the perfect way to honor Ronnie and celebrate his life.

Dad's Surprise

Mike was a mild-mannered man. His four kids would always talk about how easy going their dad was. He had a very high-level job (vice president) in the home office of a large insurance company, but he never seemed to be stressed out. Nothing would rile him. No matter what messes his kids got into growing up, he was always the calm voice of reason. When he retired three years ago, the kids were not sure what he was going to do with his time. On many occasions, they invited him to watch their kids' baseball and soccer games, and to go on school field trips. While he went on a few, he usually said he had other things to do. He went to Sunday dinners at each of their houses, and when they offered to bring him home or drop off dinners for him, he said it was too much trouble for them to drive out to his house.

When he died a short time ago, the kids all met at his house to make his final arrangements and were shocked to find that he was an artist! Apparently, he had spent the past three years painting! They had NO idea. He must have had thirty oil paintings of different sizes – small ones and large canvases, all placed throughout his entire house. They were absolutely amazing – bright colors and sunsets, seascapes, rolling hills of flowers, mountain views, and city scenes. This was certainly a part of their dad they never knew, and they decided that his art would be a part of his memorial service.

They reserved the banquet room of a local restaurant and invited all his friends and ex-co-workers, along with their family. All of Mike's paintings were displayed around the room. Light classical music was played, and a variety of appetizers, wine, and sparkling water was served. Mike's kids were proud to show everyone that their dad had an artistic side to him. Everyone was surprised, and it was a really enjoyable way to remember him.

Maya's Own Story

In Maya's Kindergarten class, story-telling was the most favorite time of the day, especially for Maya. Ms. Campbell, Maya's teacher, would have all the students sit on the "special story-telling carpet," and she would read wonderful adventurous stories of people doing daring and courageous acts. She would sometimes ask the students to create their own endings for some of the stories they had just read. And on some days, she would let one student read their own made-up story. *Everyone* had their own made up story and wanted to be chosen to read it to the class! They talked a lot about what would make a "really good story" and they decided that it had to have (1) a hero, either male or female, who was courageous, and (2) be in a magical place.

Sadly, on Christmas break, Maya was killed in a sledding accident. When the Kindergarten students returned to school and heard about Maya, they wanted to create a story for her. They each wrote their own story with Maya as the hero, and told how brave she was. Ms. Campbell sat with each student and helped each of them write their stories on large colored poster paper. She also asked them to include some drawings and artwork. When all the stories were completed, she bound them into a large "book" by stapling the left edges together.

With Maya's parents' permission, the "book" was displayed at her memorial service on a large tri-pod. Everyone who attended the service was amazed and surprised by, not only the creativity of the stories, but also of the kindness and love they felt for Maya. Her parents treasure this wonderful remembrance.

Garden Party

When Ellie was growing up she was told her Aunt Marian was "eccentric," but she always thought that she was just fun. That's why Auntie M was always Ellie's favorite aunt.

 She loved hats! Every time Ellie saw her she had on a different hat. Big ones, floppy ones, colorful ones, ones with flowers or fruit. She had them all. Ellie's grandmother (Auntie M's sister) used to roll her eyes and try to get Aunt Marian to be more "traditional," but Aunt Marian would always push the standards with her clothes, hats, and lifestyle. Ellie loved going to her house because it was a mix-match of colors and styles. There was a whole room just full of all her hats! Everyone said it was eclectic, but Ellie just thought it was fun.

Now that Ellie is in her twenties, she still appreciates Aunt Marian's unique style and realizes that her house was not so outrageously mix-matched, but that her aunt simply surrounded herself with all the things she loved (especially her hats). It didn't matter what architectural style or color anything was. As the years went by and Auntie M got older, she focused all her time on her garden. Ellie always thought it was magical, and it grew into a wonderful bouquet of beautiful flowers and colors.

When Aunt Marian died, she was very specific about her wishes. She wanted her friends and family to hold her memorial service in her garden. She requested all the female guests to wear their favorite hat. It was a wondrous sight! So

many beautiful, colorful, and crazy hats. She would have loved every minute of it.

Per her wishes, the family set up several tables through-out the garden covered with white lace tablecloths. Each table had one of her hats as a centerpiece.

A buffet of her favorite teas and small cakes were served, and Ellie handed out little velvet gift bags with Aunt Marian's favorite Ghirardelli chocolates inside (she was also a chocoholic). A large bowl of packaged flower seeds was placed in the center of the buffet table and the guests were given the opportunity to take some home to plant if they wanted. Ellie took a few packages home with her to plant in her yard and create a small "Aunt Marian Garden Spot".

Now, whenever Ellie sees a woman wearing a hat, it always brings a smile to her face. Auntie M made her realize and appreciate her own individuality, and Ellie decided that she wants her memorial service to reflect her unique person-ality. Just like her aunt.

Hawaiian Style Origami

Starting high school was an exciting time for Pualani. She knew a fair number of kids from her middle school who were also starting with her and she felt pretty good about the academic part, as she always got B's and some A's throughout elementary school. What she was really excited about was the chance to take electives.

Ever since she was little, she was fascinated with her family's Asian/Hawaiian culture. More specifically, she loved all types of Hawaiian-style origami. She was hoping to find an art class or a club where she could combine her creativity with her love of origami.

Much to her delight, there was a Polynesian Club on campus which she immediately joined. They learned and discussed different Polynesian cultures, foods, clothing, art, and history. They went on field trips to local museums and galleries to see examples of "their" art and culture. She loved high school, but she loved the Polynesian Club most of all. She taught her club members the ancient art of Hawaiian-style origami, which is a multi-step, intricate process of cutting and folding special, colorful origami paper. She showed them how to make three-dimensional designs.

In her senior year, Pualani contracted pneumococcal pneumonia. While she was in the hospital, her school friends and members of the Polynesian Club came to visit. During their visits, Pualani and her friends created origami designs and figures. They made birds, boats, flowers, cranes, geckos, fish, and even Aloha shirts. The nurses hung all the designs around her hospital room, and her window was covered with beautiful, colorful origami. You could always tell which room was Pualani's, as you could see the designs from the street!

Unfortunately, Pualani couldn't fight the infection and passed away three weeks before her high school graduation. Her parents took all of the origami designs from her hospital room and strung a "clothesline" cord from tree to tree in their front yard and hung up all the designs and figures. All summer and into the fall, if you drove by her house, you could see the colorful origami blowing in the breeze. It was a wonderful way to remember Pualani.

On the Home Front

Motown Mom

When Dwayne's mom, Loretta passed, the family had a party for her.

Loretta was born in Detroit in 1946 and grew up in the 50's. She became a teenager at the same time of Rock & Roll. Like most Baby Boomers, she loved the music: Elvis, Diana Ross and the Supremes, Chuck Berry, The Temptations, Jerry Lee Lewis, The Platters, The Ronettes, James Brown, The Four Tops; and you didn't grow up in Detroit and not love Motown! Loretta's kids grew up listening to the music and dancing in the living room.

When their grandparents passed in the 1960's, their mom and dad bought the house and never changed anything in  it. It always looks like 1954. The furniture, lamps, dishes, and the starburst clock on the wall are all from the 1950's. Today, furniture designers call it "Mid-Century Modern"; but to Dwayne and his two younger sisters, it was always home. The three kids moved out years ago, yet their mom and dad never changed one thing. Everything remained the same.

Throughout the years, Loretta's friends would come over on Saturday nights to dance in the living room. They moved the coffee table, pushed the chairs back, and danced to Motown and other 1950's songs, just like they did when they were teenagers.

When Loretta passed, the family couldn't think of a better way to celebrate her life than by having all her friends come over on a Saturday night and dance to her oldies songs in the living room. The kids set out all her favorite chips and snacks, her favorite pop to drink, and no Saturday night party would be complete without Loretta's favorite White Castle burgers!

Dwayne and his sisters are currently in the process of having her headstone engraved, and have included "Motown Mom" to the inscriptions.

The Park

Sandy grew up in southwestern Florida in a trailer park. Some people called it a mobile home park. Most of the residents just referred to it as "The Park." Sandy's mom was a single mom, and it was just the two of them since she was a baby. The Park was all Sandy knew growing up. It was a home and a neighborhood and a small little community. There was a small recreation center (a room actually, that was used for meetings, social events, craft shows, whatever), a little area that served as a playground, and a central laundry facility. They didn't need much else. The people were year-round residents who had been there for years. Sandy called the neighbors Aunt and Uncle. She had a wonderful childhood at The Park, and her high school graduation party was held in the rec center with all the neighbors (family) attending.

Sandy now lives in the "big city" of Orlando, but when her mother passed away a few months back, she immediately headed back home to The Park. Her mom was not one for fancy doings, so her memorial reception was held in the rec center. Sandy and the neighbors decided that her mom would have just wanted a simple potluck dinner with all her friends there. Sandy made her famous homemade chili, and all the neighbors brought their specialty dishes. They talked about her mom's life, her impact on the people there, and passed around a Memorial Book where each person wrote their goodbyes and things they had always wanted to say to her. The day was filled with all her mom's friends, and there was an outpouring of good food and support in honor of her.

Sandy treasures the Memorial Book. When she reads through the writings, she appreciates all the people from The Park who were part of her mother's and her life.

Nicky's Zombie Birthday Party

Kaylee's brother, Nicky, died three days before his eleventh birthday. He had been sick most of his life with a rare disease (which no one could pronounce). Just a few days earlier, the doctors said his condition seemed to have stabilized, and that if it continued to do so, he could possibly live another four to five years. That was why the family planned his Zombie-themed birthday party and sent out the party invitations.

After Nicky died unexpectedly, Kaylee's family decided to still follow through with the birthday party just as they had planned, and that it would be his memorial service as well. They added personal invitations to the nurses who knew  and cared for him. The family made it very clear that they were not going to be sad and cry, but they were going to celebrate Nicky and have fun at his party.

Everyone played all the planned party games, the magician came and did all his tricks, and the face painter painted flowers and zombies on the kid's faces. They cut his cake (the one with Zombies he wanted on it), and they all sang Happy Birthday to him.

At the end of the party, everyone took the Zombie balloons outside and let them float to Heaven so Nicky could see them. Everyone said it was a happy occasion and was so much better than a sad funeral service. The family had absolutely no regrets that they gave him a farewell birthday party. They know this would have made him happy.

Mrs. Claus

The Richardson family always goes crazy at Christmas time. For many years, their house was known for miles around as the "Christmas House" that is a must-see every year. It's been showcased in the local newspaper, and there is  usually a long line of cars waiting to cruise by and see all the displays and decorations. They have thousands of strings of lights (blinking, flashing, pulsing), continuous Christmas music playing on several speakers, hundreds of candy canes, reindeer, angels, snowflakes, wreaths, lighted garlands, snowmen and women, a Santa's Workshop with dozens of elves making their toys, and a nativity with life-size statues. They start setting it all up in October and work almost straight through to Christmas Eve. Mr. Richardson always dressed up as Santa and spent his nights out on the front lawn welcoming families and describing the history of some of his decorations (many are from the 1960's). Mrs. Richardson played Mrs. Claus and filled her mornings baking cookies so she could hand them out at night to all the kids.

When Mrs. Richardson passed away last year, the family still wanted her to be a part of the Christmas House tradition. Because they (and many of their friends and neighbors) had taken so many photos and videos of their displays over the years, they had tons of footage to choose from. They selected all the best shots of Mrs. Richardson as Mrs. Claus, and created a video of her which was projected on the front of the garage door. That way, Mrs. Richardson will always be included as part of their tradition for years to come, and her memory lives on as Mrs. Claus.

Dem Bones

She was determined to live to be 100 years old. And she did! Granny Faye lived in the small house on Walnut Street for the past 72 years. It was the house she and Mario bought when they first got married and where they raised their five children. When Mario died almost 40 years ago, her children tried to talk her into moving, but Granny Faye would have no part of that. If she moved, who would carry on the "Best Halloween House in the Neighborhood" tradition? Halloween was her and Mario's favorite holiday. Each year, they added to their collection of grave stones, bats, skeletons, and haunted house ghouls. After Mario's passing, her grandkids helped her decorate each year; and for the past several years, her daily care givers also joined in the fun. Granny Faye would sit on her porch and give them directions where to hang her skeleton collection.

Granny Faye's love for Halloween was equaled by her love of her pets. Over the years, she accumulated several cats and three dogs. For years on Halloween she would dress her pets in outrageous costumes and pass out special home-made dog bones to all the animals who came "begging". She would tell the children with dogs that the bones she was giving out were really "dem bones of the skeletons." The "dem bones" became a legend in the neighborhood. (Some still believe they are truly skeleton bones!)

She celebrated her 100th birthday in June and died peace-fully in her sleep a couple months later. The family kept her house in tact until Halloween so they could have a final Halloween party for her. They decorated her house as she liked it, dressed her cats and dogs in their costumes, and passed out her special homemade "dem bones" to all the dogs who came by. All the neighbors were invited to stop by to say their final good byes to Granny Faye and her Halloween House.

Today, the house has been sold, a new young family has moved in, but the legend of "dem bones" continues in the neighborhood.

The Dream House

When John and Lori got married thirty-four years ago, they drew up plans for their "dream house". Their first step took longer than they thought, and it took eleven years for them to buy a one-acre plot of land just outside the city limits. They also experienced many financial set-backs and delays due to job and kid-related situations, but three years ago, they finally handed over their dream house plans to an architect and contractor. Their original plan design had to be modified somewhat, but John absolutely refused to compromise on the screened in porch that extended the entire back of the house, his patio with a built-in barbeque, and an area in the backyard for his birch trees.

Sadly, John was diagnosed with pancreatic cancer almost the same day as construction of the house began. John and Lori talked it over in great detail, and with heavy hearts, they both decided to push forward with the house and not allow his medical condition to be another delay. As the house and his illness progressed, John quit his job and spent his days "supervising" the workers. He loved being a part of the building process, and Lori thought it gave him the motivation to stay strong. Once the house was finished, they had only about four months there together before John passed away.

He was very specific about his final instructions and what he wanted. He asked for his family and friends to have a small gathering on his dream patio and have a toast to him and the new house. So, even though it was the first week of November, with overcast skies and 50 degrees outside, they had a barbeque on the patio and made all of John's favorite foods. They toasted John and then spread his ashes under his birch trees. Their children were very clever. They went to the local arts & craft store and bought several packages of 6" x 9" copper sheeting. They wrote their messages to their dad on each one and poked a hole in the top. Then they hung them with wire ribbon on the branches of his birch trees.

Lori loves looking out her kitchen window every day and seeing the copper messages to John.

Part Two: The Guide

How to Create a
Personal Celebration-of-Life

How to "Go Out in Style"

The first thing you'll need when creating this plan for yourself or someone you love is an 8" x 11" folder. There are some really unique ones at most office stores that come in bright colors (rich purple, shiny black, silver, gold, emerald green, sapphire blue, garnet red, hot pink, etc.). Or look for something that catches your eye, but make sure that it is one that stands out so people will notice it if it's in your home office or sitting on a desk. If you don't want to create a hardcopy folder, just make sure all this information is on your computer or tablet and put it in a "Celebration-of-Life" file on your desktop. Be sure you write down your password.

If you choose to have a hardcopy, while at the office store, buy some heavy stock resume paper – something that is not too thick that will jam the printer, but not that skimpy, white copy paper. Select a color that will blend nicely with your folder. Or, if you like the shocking pink, glow-in-the-dark orange or lime green, go for it. Choose something that reflects *YOU* or for whomever you are creating this plan.

Now, it's time to write the plan. Do not worry about writing this. It's not a thesis or a doctoral dissertation. This plan should only end up to be about 7 to 9 pages total – possibly more pages, depending on how many friends and family members you want to include.

Writing the Plan

Think about planning this Celebration-of-Life event or Send-off Celebration just as you would plan a wedding, an anniversary party, or any other life celebration. The same factors and concepts apply:

- Think about *who* to invite – family (both close and extended, even those who haven't been seen in years), friends, business associates, neighbors, etc.

- *How* you will invite them – phone, internet, E-vite, email, social media (Twitter, Facebook, etc.), regular mail.

- *Where* to hold this event – someone's house, restaurant, park, social club, church basement, sports bar or tavern, etc.

- What will be *served* – breakfast, brunch, lunch, dinner (sit down or family-style, buffet or food stations), or a cocktail party serving only appetizers or snacks.

- Other "ambience" such as decorations, centerpieces, props, flowers, photos, music, etc., even remembrance items, mementos, and give-a-ways.

Page One: The Obituary Page

Who better to write this than you? Why would you let your spouse, spousal equivalent, partner, or children write something so important when they are in a serious emotional state right after your death? Are they in the right frame of mind to remember your jobs, associations, and important dates and places? Take this emotional task away from them and write it yourself or fill it out with your loved one. This is not a difficult task. There are templates to help; just fill in the blanks and change the names and places to fit you or your loved one's life.

This book provides three "standard" obituary formats: (1) "Basic," (2) "Enhanced," and (3) "Premium." These templates were taken from a large metropolitan city newspaper and should be accepted by most city or local newspapers. Check with your newspaper for costs. If you don't read or get a newspaper, use this format to help you write an article for your Facebook page or other social media.

The BASIC

Last Name, First Name

John Doe, 72, of Phoenix, Arizona, passed away on June 28, 2014. He served in the US Navy. Memorial service will be held at 100 E. Washington Street, Phoenix, Arizona 85012 on June 30, 2014 from 2:00 to 3:00 p.m. with a one-hour visitation prior to the service in the Hall of Serenity. Contributions can be made to a favorite charity of your choice. Arrangements by ABC Funeral Home.

The ENHANCED

Last Name, First Name

John Doe of Phoenix, Arizona, passed away on June 28, 2014 at the age of 72. John Doe was born and raised in Seattle, Washington. John is survived by his wife Jane Doe and his three children: Jill Doe, Justin Doe, and Jason Doe. John is also survived by his brother Joe and sister Jan. Memorial services will be held at 100 E. Washington Street, Phoenix, Arizona 85012 on June 30, 2014 from 2:00 to 3:00 p.m. with a one-hour visitation prior to the service in the Hall of Serenity. Arrangements by ABC Funeral Home. The family suggests donations be made to a favorite charity of your choice. Rest in Peace John; you will be truly missed.

The PREMIUM w/Photo

Last Name, First Name

John Doe of Phoenix, Arizona, passed away on June 28, 2014 at the age of 72. John Doe was born and raised in Seattle, Washington. John is survived by his wife Jane Doe and his three children: Jill Doe, Justin Doe, and Jason Doe. John is also survived by his brother Joe and his sister Jan. John served in the US Navy for 15 years and was stationed in Bremerton, Washington. After leaving the Navy, John went to Arizona State University and received a degree in engineering. He then became a semiconductor engineer at XYZ Inc. He was a volunteer at the local high school and was very active in his local community. John was an avid golfer and loved to play the local valley courses. John will be missed by his golfing buddies, his pals at The Club, his family, and all who knew him. Memorial services will be held at 100 E. Washington Street, Phoenix, Arizona 85012 on June 30, 2014 from 2:00 to 3:00 p.m. with a one-hour visitation prior to the service in the Hall of Serenity. Arrangements by ABC Funeral Home. The family suggests donations be made to a favorite charity of your choice. Rest in Peace John; you will be truly missed.

Once the Obituary is completed, print it out and put it in the folder. Or, label the electronic file and put it in your e-folder.

Page Two: The List of Favorite Songs

We grew up with music and we should go out with music.

Music has been a large part of many of our lives. This will be a list of all favorite songs that will be played during the celebration-of-life event. *Do not* leave this up to your spouse, spousal equivalent, partner, or children. They may *think* they know what you like, but they do not know the specifics. (I asked my daughters if they knew what music I would like to have at my send-off celebration and they said, "Of course, we know. You like the Oldies." And they were insulted that I didn't think they knew that. But, I said, "That's two decades – 20 years' worth of songs! Which specific ones would you pick?" And when they just looked at each other, I knew I had to choose the songs myself. It would be just my luck that they picked out the few songs I hated. Besides, I also have a lot of favorite country and R&B songs.

Go to an internet search engine – Google, Bing, or whatever, and type in "the top 100 songs of: the 1940's, 1950's, 60's, 70's, 80's, 90's, 2000's", or "the top Country, Jazz, Religious, Gospel, Classical or R&B songs." Once you get the lists of the top songs, then you or you and your loved one can pick out all of the favorites and make a list. It's fine if you end up with about 15 or 20 songs, as they will be playing throughout the send-off celebration. Type the list, print it out, and add to the folder.

Page Three: The Photos

This is not really a page, but a place holder for photos. It is the job of you, or you with your loved one, to choose the photo that will be attached to the obituary, placed on a stand next to the casket, or set on a table near a sign-in book, etc. Do not let your spouse, spousal equivalent, partner, or children make this decision. They will all argue about it, as each one would prefer their favorite photo. You or your loved one should choose the one to be used.

When my friend Brian died, his children chose a 1980's photo of him with a mustache. None of his friends of the last fifteen years even recognized him! My friend Barb was always embarrassed by what she called her "skinny, chicken legs." Her children placed a full-length photo of her on the easel next to her casket. She would have hated that photo.

Go back to the office store and buy a clear 8" x 11" report cover or sleeve (the ones students put their hardcopy reports in to give to their teachers). Or, a regular 8" x 11" envelope will work as well; just make sure it fits in your folder. Photocopy or scan the chosen obit photo and label it "Obit Photo" on the back. Then go through all the framed photos, scrapbooks, and computer or on-line photo galleries, and choose all the photos you think represents you or your loved one's life.

Choose a couple of photos from each of the stages of life: as a baby; childhood and growing up; in high school (graduation and/or prom); the wedding; the family (nucleus and extended); photos of hobbies or favorite things to do (fishing, golfing, swimming, traveling, etc.) Family and friends would like to see you/your loved one all throughout life. Maybe some people didn't know you or your loved one as a child, and they will take pleasure in seeing all the life stages.

Take all these photos and copy or scan them and put them in the clear report cover or envelope for your folder. You can also save them to a "thumb" drive.

If you would like, you can combine your music and photo choices on a CD or thumb drive. If you do not have the technological skills to do this, at least you have the basics of what is needed for someone else to do this.

Page Four: The Actual Plan

This is where all the preferences are described for the service. There is a whole series of survey questions to answer and decisions to be made. You might want to print out these questions and put the answers on each page to keep as a reference.

Do you, or your loved one, want:

1) A religious, church, chapel, synagogue, or faith-based service?

    a) If yes, which one?

    b) Where is it located?

2) A service in a funeral home or mortuary?

    a) If yes, which one?

    b) Where is it located?

3) Do you want a religious service and then a separate funeral service at a funeral home?

4) Do you want a full religious service? A long or short memorial service?

5) Do you have a specific priest, pastor, minister, etc. to officiate the service?

6) Do you want any family or friends to speak at the service?

7) Do you want to be in a casket or cremated? Check online for the latest options in caskets and cremation vessels.

    a) If in a casket: What type of material? Metal? Wood? Stone? Ceramic? Or reeds and other materials found in nature? Do you want any special designs (flowers, angels), emblems (military, sports teams), signs (for example, Zodiac) on your casket? There are lots of very unique choices with caskets.

    b) If cremated: Do you want your ashes in an urn to be buried? Displayed? Or spread somewhere?

    c) What type of urn do you want? There is a huge selection of urns – those to be buried, and those to be displayed. Choices range from engraved boxes, containers shaped like footballs or baseballs, music boxes, or jewelry (ashes placed in a locket, bracelet, or ring).

8) Do you want any flowers? If yes, which kind? A lot? Small bouquet?

9) Do you want any special songs or hymns at the service? If yes, which ones? Anyone in particular to sing? If so, who?

10) Do you want any food to be served at this service? Cookies, small finger food, fruit and cheeses? Or a buffet? A barbeque?

11) Do you want this service to take place at any particular time of day?

12) Do you want a gravesite service?

    a)   If yes, which cemetery? Where is it located?

    b)   Do you want everyone to come or just family and close friends?

    c)   Do you want the big procession of cars or everyone to just meet there?

13) Do you want any memorial or holy cards to be passed out?

    a)   If holy card, which saint or holy person? Any particular prayer?

    b)   If a memorial card, do you want your obit photo on it? Do you want a prayer or blessing on it? What size? A single card, a double or tri-fold?

14) Do you want any other giveaways? One option is a "goodie bag." If you are addicted to chocolate-covered raisins, make a note that you want small baggies (such as a net bag, colorful gift bag, or small jewelry bag) full of something for your guests to take home in remembrance of you.

This may seem like an incredibly huge amount of decisions to be made, but it all should boil down to just one page of your preferences. (See the Appendix for an example.) Type out the preferences and put it in your folder.

Page Five: The Specifics

This page explains exactly how to "Go Out in Style" for you or someone you love. It's your memorial. Your personal Celebration-of-Life. Your personalized Send-off Celebration. This also should be about one page. This is where the event is truly personalized. A lot of fun can be had here. Now here are more questions to be answered and decisions to be made.

Decide the *where*. Choose a place that represents you or your loved one's life. Will this event be:

Inside:

- At a home – your home, your friend's, child's, or other relative's home
- At your favorite restaurant, bar, grille, ice cream parlor, hotel, etc.
- At a club where you are a member – a private club, golf/tennis club, a country club, a service club (Lions, Jaycee's, Veterans, VFW, etc.)
- At a church social hall, basement, facility

Outside:

- In a garden, at your local botanical gardens
- At the park or your favorite picnic grounds
- At home, but on the patio or backyard
- At the beach
- On the mountain or your favorite hiking trail

Decide the *food*.

- Will there be any food served? If yes, what kind: breakfast, brunch, lunch, dinner, appetizers, snacks, desserts?
- Do you/your loved one want this to be a sit-down meal or a buffet, or do you want "food stations" or a barbeque?
- Or, do you want a cocktail party?

This is the opportunity to create a party and serve all your or your loved one's favorite foods, snacks, desserts, and drinks. My friend Suz has already written down that she wants to serve all the foods she was allergic to throughout most of her life – peanuts, ice cream, shrimp, and wine!

Other *requests:* This is also the place to make requests of your guests. Would you/your loved one like the guests to wear anything specific: big hats, baseball caps, sport team jerseys, something purple or pink (or whatever your favorite color is).

Decide *props, giveaways and goodie bag items*. Be specific about what to use or give away. Goodie bags and giveaways are wonderful mementos to give to friends and family. A man who loved to play poker and gamble had a pair of dice and a poker chip with his name printed on it in his goodie bags. Personalized table centerpieces are also fun: fancy hats, cowboy boots, old sports trophies, etc. Don't be afraid to say what you want because everyone will love the props!

See the example and type out your or your loved one's preference event and put it in your folder.

Page Six: The Invitation

The invitation should state where the Celebration-of-Life event is to take place, the address and time. It also could include who is hosting the event and what is being served. If you want guests to wear or bring something, include it in the invitation. Print out a sample invitation for your folder.

An Optional Page Seven: The Readings/ Poems, etc.

Another page can be added if you or your loved one would like to include any copies of spiritual or other readings, poems, blessings, etc. Print out a copy of what is wanted, and put it in the folder. That way, there will be no misunderstandings. Document if these readings are to take place during the service, or only printed on the memorial card.

The last and final page is a list of all requested attendees.

Simply print out your or your loved one's email distribution list or copy your/their address, phone book or Holiday/ Christmas card list, and add it to your folder. This can include phone numbers and/or email addresses – whichever way someone can connect or reach the people you or your loved one wants to be at your service and Celebration-of-Life event. This can be one page, or many. It all depends on how many family and friends to include.

Appendix

Example of a Personalized
Celebration-of-Life Plan

Celebration
Of Life

John L. Doe

Born September 20, 19XX
Died June 28, 20XX

John's Obituary Preference:

Doe, John:

John Doe of Phoenix, Arizona, passed away on June 28, 20xx at the age of 68. John Doe was born in Seattle, Washington and moved to Phoenix when he was 12. John graduated from Central High School and served in the US Navy for 15 years, stationed in Bremerton, Washington. After leaving the Navy, John went to Arizona State University and received a degree in engineering. He then became a semiconductor engineer at XYZ Inc. He was a volunteer at the local high school and was very active in his local community. John was an avid golfer and loved to play the local valley courses. John is survived by his wife Jane Doe and his three children: Jill Doe, Justin Doe, and Jason Doe, along with two grandchildren Jackson and Jenna. John is also survived by his brother Joe and sister Jan. Memorial services will be held at 100 E. Washington Street, Phoenix, Arizona on June 30, 20xx from 2:00 to 3:00 pm with a one-hour visitation prior to the service in the Hall of Serenity. John was well liked and respected by all who knew him; he will be truly missed.

John's Music Preferences:

- *Amazing Grace*, Chris Tomlin
- *Jailhouse Rock*, Elvis Presley
- *Hunk of Burning Love*, Elvis Presley
- *Chattahoochee*, Alan Jackson
- *Blue Suede Shoes*, Carl Perkins
- *I Walk the Line*, Johnny Cash
- *Whole Lotta Shakin' Goin' On*, Jerry Lee Lewis
- *Take the A Train*, Duke Ellington
- *Lucille*, Little Richard
- *Your Cheatin' Heart*, Hank Williams
- *Rebel Rouser*, Duane Eddy
- *Stand by Me,* Ben E. King
- *Wild Thing*, Troggs
- *Wish You Were Here*, Pink Floyd
- *Heroes*, David Bowie
- *Blue Train*, John Coltrane
- *Old Time Rock 'n' Roll*, Bob Seger
- *Ain't too Proud to Beg*, Temptations
- *How Great is Our Lord*, Chris Tomlin
- *Born to be Wild*, Steppenwolf
- *Ring of Fire*, Johnny Cash
- *I Feel Good*, James Brown
- *Proud Mary*, Credence Clearwater Revival
- *He Will Carry Me*, Mark Schultz

John's Service Preferences

I would like a short service (no more than 45 minutes) at the Mission Bible Church on Central Avenue and Camelback Road; the time preference is mid-afternoon. If Pastor Charles is still around, that would be nice if he would preside. If my wife, Jane, my children, my grandchildren, or any of my friends would like to say a few words at this service, that's their choice, but not required or necessary.

Please pass out the poem cards I have chosen. I would like the poem cards to have my obit photo on the front and the Irish Blessing on the back.

No funeral home, mortuary or casket please; and no cemetery plot or cemetery procession and burial service. I prefer cremation with my ashes placed in a golf-related urn (you all can choose the one you like the best) to be given to my wife Jane.

Not too many flowers; it's not a good use of anyone's money. Instead, donations can be sent to The American Cancer Society. And no food served after this service. I want a separate memorial celebration to be held at another time.

John's Memorial

Celebration-of-Life Preferences

I would like my Celebration-of-Life party to be held at Mickey's Sports Bar on Central Avenue some week night during Happy Hour (5–7pm) after my death.

I would like my three children to host this party using the money I have put aside for this. Find the taped yellow envelope in the back of my top right dresser drawer. Please serve all my favorite snacks and foods at Mickey's – potato chips, popcorn, pretzels, and Mickey's famous sub sandwich. Also serve Mickey's special draft beer. Invite all the folks I've listed on the attendee list. Don't forget to include all my golf buddies. Be sure there is enough food and drinks for everyone.

I would like the DVD with my chosen photos and music preferences to be played during this time. Ask Mickey for help setting this up. Make sure everyone knows the dress is casual.

John's Poem Preference

(This poem is to be printed on one side of my poem card, the obit photo on the other side.)

Irish Blessing

May the road rise to meet you

May the wind be always at your back

May the sun shine warm upon your face

And the rains fall soft upon your fields

Until we meet again

~ Author Unknown

John's Event Invitation

John Doe passed away on June 28, 20xx

You are invited to

John's Send-Off Celebration

On Thursday, July 1st

from 5:00 to 7:00 p.m.

at Mickey's Sports Bar

160 N. Central Ave

Hosted by his friends Doug Stall, Cal Winters, Rob

McCormick, & Sean Forbes

And his children Jill, Justin, and Jason

We will be serving John's favorite snacks,

Mickey's famous sub sandwich,

And John's favorite beer –

Mickey's special draft

Dress is casual

Please come and celebrate John's life with us.

Attendees

Jill Doe and Ray Costa, jcosta@gmail.com

Justin and Susie Doe, jandsdoe@att.net, 602-555-9090

Jason Doe, jasonplumbingphx@yahoo.com

Joe Doe, 12235 N. 7th St. Phoenix, 85003, 602-555-8976

Jan and Bill Cunningham, jcc@gmail.com

Alexander and Mimi Doe, 819 W. 1st Ave.

Aaron, Jodi and Joey Doe, Maricopa, 520-555-2215

Doug and Krissy Stall, 56678 W. Indian School, 602-555-6790

Cal and Rita Winters, 480-555-8765

Robert McCormick and Katy Miles, robertmc12@att.net

Sean and Debbie Forbes, 670 E. McDowell #23

Neighbors Pam and Brian Cipriani, 602-555-9876

Neighbors Edna and Roger Lindberg, 602-555-5401

Denny and Ruth Turner, drturner@yahoo.com

Cameron, Julie, Taylor, Carly and Carsyn Haley, haleyfamily@gmail.com

Stephanie Marlow, 33499 Pearson, Gilbert, AZ

Dr. and Mrs. Gene Flannigan, 602-555-7621

Friends at Mickey's – see Mickey Flynn for "regulars" 602-555-6543

Friends at Rockney's Barber Shop on Central and Palm, 602-555-0021

Golf friends via Rich Vandy, 602-555-8906

About the Author

For over 30 years, Susan Opalka's professional career was in market research and marketing. Her responsibilities were to analyze market conditions, new trends and directions; to identify target markets; to understand consumers' behavior and motivations; and to understand the competitive environment. Over the years she has conducted hundreds of large, quantitative research studies, moderated hundreds of focus groups and one-on-one interviews. Her focus was on the anthropological and social aspects of business marketing.

She worked at Foote, Cone, Belding Advertising Agency in San Francisco in the research department aiding clients such as Levi's and Clorox. For five years, she identified target markets and new product opportunities for Apple Computer. In Arizona, she was the Marketing Research Manager at APS, the Director of Competitive Intelligence at Motorola, and the Marketing/Market Research Director at Sage Software.

Ms. Opalka has a Bachelor's Degree in Sociology and a Master's Degree in Public Administration. She also taught graduate-level classes in marketing, market research, consumer behavior, new product development, and organizational leadership at Keller Graduate School of Management for over twenty years.

Since her retirement, Susan has continued her interest in ethnography, generational marketing, and monitoring social trends and new directions.

Note: All the stories in this book are directly related to personal experiences of the author.

Submit Your Own Story!

Do YOU have a story to tell? Have you attended or planned a unique or non-traditional Celebration-of-Life event? If you would like to share your experience, please send me your story. If chosen, your story may be published in Volume Two of *Going Out in Style*. If your story is chosen, I may have to take some liberties with names, places, and writing style; but your first name and city will be mentioned and acknowledged. Please understand that you are giving me your story free of charge and giving up your rights to publish it yourself. But think of the huge audience who will read it!

Thank you,

Susan Opalka

www.goingoutinstylebook.com

Send stories via email to: susanopalka@yahoo.com